T0381178

Mather's Theological
Compendium III

Dennis Mather

WESTBOW
PRESS®
A DIVISION OF THOMAS NELSON
& ZONDERVAN

WestBow Press books may be ordered through booksellers or by contacting:

WestBow Press
A Division of Thomas Nelson & Zondervan
1663 Liberty Drive
Bloomington, IN 47403
www.westbowpress.com
844-714-3454

ISBN: 979-8-3850-3313-3 (sc)
ISBN: 979-8-3850-3314-0 (e)

Library of Congress Control Number: 2024919818

Print information available on the last page.

WestBow Press rev. date: 10/09/2024

PREFACE

The treatises in this book were written in the last five years, with the exception of two term papers that were written for a Psalms class at Faith Baptist Bible College and Seminary. Those two treatises were written in 1976.

I began this book with a treatise that explains where we are in local church history. It is chapter one of part one.

But then in chapter two I explain why Israel is a part of the kingdom of God and why she is important to Jesus Christ, just as important as His Church.

However, there is a third part of the Kingdom of God that is as important and loved by Jesus. I explain this in detail in section one also.

In part two I have included the two treatises that were written in 1976. They give further light about the nation of Israel.

And lastly, I end with two short stories about Christians who are doing 'God's work' in today's world. It is part three of this book.

So I began writing about the local church and end writing about it. We need to be building the local church (Matthew 16:16-19; 1 Timothy 3:15), because it helps our Lord build His real Church, the church that includes everyone who is born again. It is called the Church Universal (or, the Body of Christ) and includes all saved people from the day of Pentecost to the rapture of the Church.

PART ONE

Doctrinal Treatises About Things I've Been Thinking About

CHAPTER ONE
A Reformation

God is doing something big in the world, and it is bigger than a revival. This is because we are in the midst of a reformation, and it has come about because of the apostasy of the Sardis church, the Sardis church being the fifth local church mentioned in chapters two and three of the book of Revelation.

In *Mather's Theological Compendium*[1] I discussed the seven churches of Revelation, chapters two and three. They are seven churches located in ancient Asia Minor, which is today the country of Turkey.[2]

These seven churches have two applications for us to take into consideration. number one is that they are examples of not only how to live for Jesus Christ, but also how not to live for Him, which will be seen when reading chapters two and three of the book of Revelation.

They are also, as application number two, a running

---

[1] *Mather's Theological Compendium* (West Bow Press, Bloomington, IN) -2014.

[2] The seven churches are: 1.) Ephesus; 2.) Smyrna; 3.) Pergamum; 4.) Thyatira; 5.) Sardis; 6.) Philadelphia and 7.) Laodicea.

history of the local church that God has sanctioned because Jesus holds them in His hand (Revelation 1:4c, 12b-13a, 16a, 20; 3:1b). They exist for the purpose of not only fellowship and instruction for the believer, but also for winning the lost to Christ. So, the local church in our day and age is still very important.

And this reformation that is happening before our very eyes equals the likes of what Martin Luther started back in 1517, and is found in Revelation, chapter three where the flow of the text changes from the church in Sardis to the church in Philadelphia. And it is where Sardis is reprimanded for being "dead" (3:1c), and where the Philadelphia church is commended for keeping Jesus' word (3:8). It also commends the Philadelphia church for the fact that they have not "denied" Jesus' name (also found in Revelation 3:8).

I say this because it is evident that in our towns and cities there is a "dead" church every ten blocks or so, and there is also in these towns and cities churches that praise Jesus with every ounce of their being. And some of these "Praise Churches" are big, very big, because people are flocking to them. And people are flocking to them because they are preaching the truth about how Jesus Christ is "the way, the truth and the life." (John 14:6).

You can also tell these churches are Philadelphia churches, because when they come out of the mainline denominations they usually change their names on the signs in front of their buildings.

So, the Philadelphia "lampstand" is in the forefront now (read Revelation, chapters 1-3, especially 1:20; 2:1,5 and 3:1,8). This means Sardis' lampstand has been replaced which is what happened to Ephesus in Revelation chapter two, verse five.

This also means the Sardis church has become a Laodicean church.

But there is a difference between our present reformation and the one 500 years ago in that on the most part, it is whole congregations that are coming out and being separate. However, individual believers must find these 'praise churches' and get themselves involved. And it is also individual believers that must show the love that is necessary toward the people who are making the switch, so they will feel welcome in our churches.

Another difference is that this present reformation is world-wide, instead of just in Europe, as the reformation in the 16th century was. However, Luther's reformation did spread later to other places in the world by missionary effort.

Right now, all the time, I hear of people starting new churches, and they are praising the Lord with exuberance. And lots of them are in places where they must be underground. But they are excelling mightily due to the fact they are called to do so (Rev. 3:8b)!

CHAPTER TWO
God's Wife

The Olive Tree is God's Wife, and it is found in Romans 11:11-24 and Psalm 52:8.

The Olive Tree is also known as the Kingdom of God and pertains to the way things will be in the future when the Church and Israel will be one entity. It must be this way, because God is not polygamous (Hosea 2:16).

And what do I mean by "God is not polygamous?" It is that Israel is referred to as God's wife in Isaiah 54:5, Hosea 2:16 and Jeremiah 3:14. But it also must be remembered that we, the born-again Church, are "the Bride of Christ" (John 3:29-30; 2 Corinthians 11:2; Revelation 19:7). So someday the two of us will be one, because God believes in monogamy.

But the Olive Tree will have three parts, just as we as humans have three parts, the body, the soul and the spirit. This corresponds to how we were created in God's image, who is a Trinity and has three parts: the Father, the Son and the Holy Spirit.

So God's wife has three parts. They are: 1.) the Church; 2.) Israel and 3.) those who were righteous

Gentiles and lived either before the Church age or will be living after the Church age. So these righteous Gentiles are not part of the Church, and they are not part of Israel either.

They include the godly line of Seth (Genesis, chapters 4, 5 and 6), who is the third son of Adam and Eve, and the righteous Gentiles include those who are martyred during the Tribulation and are under the alter (Revelation 6:9). And thirdly, righteous Gentiles include all others who are saved from among the Gentile nations who are not part of the Church, or Israel, such as Naman, the Syrian general, Rahab, the harlot and the city of Ninevah. Also, they include those Gentiles who are going to be saved during the Millennium.

In Romans 11:16-24 we see a "grafting in" process where the Church is being grafted into the Olive tree, the root of the Olive tree being Jesus Christ.

We also see in the Old Testament where Israel will be grafted back into the Olive Tree (Isaiah 54:4-8).

And this grafting back in process also includes those Gentiles that were mentioned earlier.

There is, however, a false doctrine saying that the Church has replaced the Jewish Nation in God's eyes and mind. But this is not so. They are still "God's Chosen People" just as we in the born-again-Church are His "Chosen People" (1 Peter 1:1-2; 1 Timothy 3:14–15; Romans 9:23-24; Colossians 1:18; Matthew 18:20; Luke 14:23; Hebrews 10:25)

And, of course, the righteous Gentiles just mentioned are "God's Chosen People". It is just that we are all going to be "grafted into" the Olive Tree someday.

CHAPTER THREE
New Jerusalem

In the future, citizens of the Olive Tree are going to be living in New Jerusalem for all of eternity. Some of them are there already and are the righteous Gentiles[3] who went to Heaven when Jesus took them there in Ephesians 4, verses 8 to 10. That passage of scripture read as follows in the New international version:

> [8] This is why it says:
> 'When he ascended on high, he took many captives and gave gifts to his people.'
> (What does 'he ascended' mean except that he also descended to the lower, earthly regions. [10] He who descended is the very one who ascended higher than all the heavens, in order to fill the whole universe.)

However, people who have died "in Jesus" during

---

[3] In 1 Peter 3:18-20, Peter indicates that Jesus preached to these people by means of the Holy spirit after He was crucified.

the Church dispensation (John 14:1-3; John 1:12; Revelation 3:20), and died before the rapture of the Church are in a holding place near New Jerusalem (Revelation 6:9).[4] So, it seems that those who have died in Christ are living (or sleeping) in a certain place and must wait for the rapture of the Church to receive new glorified bodies. But it will be just about two days that we must wait since a thousand years on earth is as a day in Heaven (2 Peter 3:8).

And what kind of a body does everybody have that lives in New Jerusalem? The kind found in Philippians, chapter three, verses 20 and 21. It reads as follows:

> [20] But our citizenship is in heaven. And we eagerly await a Savior from there, the Lord Jesus Christ, [21] who, by the power that enables him to bring everything under his control, will transform our lowly bodies so that they will be like his glorious body.

But it is at the Rapture of the Church that all born-again Christians receive their glorified bodies (1 Corinthians 15:51-52; 1 Thessalonians 4:13-17).

---

[4] Those who have died in Christ, and their bodies are sleeping (Matthew 9:24; Mark 5:39; Luke 8:52; John 11:11; 1 Corinthians 15:51; 1 Thessalonians 4:5, 6, 14), are "under the alter" (Revelation 6:9).

CHAPTER FOUR
Raptures Are Big

Do we all realize how big, really big, the Rapture of the Church will be? It is amazing how every born-again Christian that ever lived, and those living at the time, will be raptured, or raised at once in the "twinkling of an eye." (1 Corinthians 15:51-52; 1 Thessalonians 4:13-17). It has been determined that a twinkling is 1/16 of a blink, so it will be fast!

There are those who say that God, at the Rapture, creates for us a new body by immediate creation, or creation out of nothing.[5] However, the apostle Paul in 1 Corinthians, chapter 15 says that, it is by mediate creation, or a creation from another source than direct creation from the Lord. This means it is from a seed that these bodies are created, and is why Paul said, "it is sown a natural body, it is raised a spiritual body" (1 Corinthians 15:44). He also said this after a lesson on seeds being sown and the plant coming to life as the same plant as the seed that was sown. (However, 1

---

[5] See the work by Charles Hodge entitled *Mediate and Immediate Creation* at: https://www.ccel/hodge/theology1.iv.x.ii.html.

Corinthians 15:38 does say that the Lord gets artistically creative!)

The passage in 1 Corinthians 15:35-38 and 42-44 that describes this in detail reads as follows in the New International version:

> [35] But someone will ask, "How are the dead raised? With what kind of body will they come?" [36] How foolish! What you sow does not come to life unless it dies. [37] When you sow, you do not plant the body that will be, but just a seed, perhaps of wheat or of something else. [38] But God gives it a body as he has determined, and to each kind of seed he gives its own body. . . .
>
> [42] So will it be with the resurrection of the dead. The body that is sown is perishable, it is raised imperishable; [43] it is sown in dishonor, it is raised in glory; it is sown in weakness, it is raised in power; [44] it is sown a natural body, it is raised a spiritual body.
>
> If there is a natural body, there is also a spiritual body.

This means God can find any cell of everybody who has died in Christ, and He can find the DNA in every nucleus of these cells.

And I think it is this DNA that is raised to a new body (1 Corinthians 15:42-44) as a mediate creation, or a creation from the same source (1 Corinthians 15:49).

And God can find one cell of millions of people,

which means He knows where every one of them is, whether they are buried in the ground, buried at sea or cremated. And He can plant the seed for a new body for everybody if they have accepted Jesus Christ as their personal savior (Revelation 3:20; John 1:12).

And 2 Corinthians 5:6-9 says that to be absent from the body is to be present with the Lord.

However, I previously pointed out in footnote number four that everyone who has died in Christ has a body that is sleeping. And I think it is everyone's DNA that is sleeping, so after we have all been raptured, we will have glorious spiritual bodies in Heaven that are received at the rapture of the Church (1 Thessalonians 4:13-17).

CHAPTER FIVE

After the Rapture of the Church

After the Rapture of the Church, we are only betrothed to Jesus Christ, as we are now. The wedding ceremony comes at the end of the Millennium when Israel has finally made herself ready (Revelation 19:7,8; 21:2,3).

To understand why Revelation 19:7 appears to be chronologically out of order, but is not, we must understand the Jewish wedding process when Jesus was here on earth. That process started with a betrothal that lasted for an undetermined amount of time, and this started for us when we accepted Jesus Christ as our personal savior.

After the rapture of the Church, however, we know that the betrothal to Jesus will last for another 1007 years. But that's OK because we will be in Heaven, and in Heaven, time is determined much differently because of 2 Peter 3:8.

We don't leave Heaven with Jesus, as some think, to help with His second coming. That is the ping-pong theory, and those are angels that follow Jesus to the

Battle of Armageddon (Matthew 13:30,39-42,48-50; 25:31; 2 Thessalonians 1:7).

The Bible says we will "ever be with the Lord," in 1 Thessalonians 4:17, so we never leave Heaven once we are there and will be living in New Jerusalem forever. (That is after sleeping for a couple of days, or hours, in that holding place!)

And scripture indicates that some people will sit with Him on thrones during the Millennium (Matthew 19:28; 1 Corinthians 6:3,4; Revelation 20:4).[6] But it is just those who are appointed to do so that will be sitting on these thrones (Revelation 20:4; Matthew 19:28).

---

[6] I have come to the conclusion that Revelation 3:21 will be for us as Christians on the New Earth as we are living in the New Jerusalem.

CHAPTER SIX

Israelites are Resurrected in Daniel 12:1-3, But are Raptured Later

The resurrection that is seen in Daniel, chapter twelve, verses one to three is just that, a resurrection. It is not a rapture, because a rapture gives people a glorified spiritual body fit for Heaven.

This resurrection is for righteous Israelites that have died up to when the Millennium starts and gives them bodies fit for the Millennium. It includes 1.) the patriarchs such as Abraham, Isaac and Jacob and their offspring, 2.) the Israelites who lived in Goshe who ended up as slaves, and 3.) it includes the established nation of Israel in the Old Testament. The righteous Israelites that will die during the Great Tribulation are included, also.[7]

---

[7] I think Messianic Jews who have accepted Christ during the Church age will be a part of the born-again Church and will be raptured when it is raptured. They have given up their old selves and have accepted Jesus Christ as their savior to have a new life in Him (Romans 6:8; Galatians 2:20; Ephesians 4:21-24; Colossians 1:27; 1 Peter 1:23). This is what members of the born-again Church have done.

This resurrection in Daniel twelve will happen so that all Israelites will have natural resurrection bodies for the Millennium. And some of them will receive those rewards for sitting on thrones with Jesus (Revelation 20:4, 6).

And it is evident in Daniel 12:1-3 that gifts are given, especially in verse three. The Daniel 12:1-3 passage reads as follows,

> [1]"At that time Michael, the great prince who protects your people, will arise. There will be a time of distress such as has not happened from the beginning of nations until then. But at that time your people—everyone whose name is found written in the book—will be delivered. [2] Multitudes who sleep in the dust of the earth will awake: some to everlasting life, others to shame and everlasting contempt. [3] Those who are wise will shine like the brightness of the heavens, and those who lead many to righteousness, like the stars for ever and ever.

Those who are resurrected in the Daniel 12:1,2 resurrection does not include everyone who will go into the Millennium from the Great Tribulation (Matthew 13:30), because these people are still alive. This includes the 144,000 of Revelation, chapter seven, and it also includes the remnant that was hidden out in the wilderness (Revelation 12:6,14).

A resurrection is necessary because righteous

Israelites who have died up to this time, as you remember, are sleeping in the earth and have yet to receive natural resurrection bodies which everyone has during the Millennium for which to make a living for themselves (Isiah 65:18-25).

So the Daniel 12:1-3 resurrection is only a resurrection, because these people are not raptured up to Heaven; instead, they go into the Millennium.

However, in the next chapter I will discuss the rapture that all righteous Israelites will participate in.

CHAPTER SEVEN
The Three Raptures

I have found three raptures in scripture, and during each of them everyone receives a 'glorified spiritual body' (1 Corinthians 15:50-54; Revelation 21:5,6).

The first rapture is the one that is found in Ephesians 4:8-10; the second one is the rapture of the Church, and the third rapture is the I Am Making Everything New Rapture which is right after the Millennium. And to be raptured means everyone who has been given the privilege of participating in it are given their glorified spiritual bodies!

Rewards are also given at all these raptures, the same as after the rapture of the Church. This means every time there is a rapture, there are rewards given at a 'bema seat,'[8] the 'bema seat' for Christians being the Judgment Seat of Christ (2 Corinthians 5:10).

The giving of rewards is especially seen in Ephesians 4:8, although in that instance, the passage has a double application. This means it can also apply

---

[8] When Olympians stand on that platform with their awards around their necks with the gold metal winner's national anthem being played, the platform is called a 'bema seat'.

to Jesus giving the Church gifts because of the context that it is found in.[9]

This rapture that is found in Ephesians 4, verses 7 to ten is where Jesus took the righteous Gentiles in Paradise (Matthew 12:38, 39; Luke 16:19-31) to Heaven, because He preached to them as it says in 1 Peter 3:18-20. He took them to Heaven because they were eligible due to His sacrifice for them on Calvay's cross. However, even though Jesus made the way to Heaven for all of the past righteous people of the nation of Israel and canceled all their sins, they must wait until after the Millennium to receive their glorified bodies.

So it is at the wedding of the Lamb after the Millennium that God finishes grafting everyone into the Olive Tree (Isiah 54:5; Revelation 21:2-6).

This means it is the Church, the nation of Israel, as well as righteous Gentiles of all ages, who make up a complete bride for Jesus Christ. And this will include Gentiles who lived and were also born during the Millennium that have accepted King Jesus as their personal savior right along with Israelites who lived and were also born during the Millennium and accepted King Jesus as their personal savior. They, along with everyone resurrected in Daniel 12:1-3, are raptured to Heaven after the Millennium in order to receive a glorified body for living there.[10]

Them a new heaven and new earth are created

---

[9] There are five gifts found in Ephesians, chapter four that are included in the 21 spiritual gifts that are in the New Testament. (See the original *Mather's Theological Compendium* for a synopsis of them.)

[10] This means Gentiles are also included in the "I Am Making Everything New" rapture!

(Revelation 21:1) after the old heaven and old earth are destroyed (2 Peter 3:10-13) due to the fact they are utterly defiled by sin (Romans 1:21-32; 2 Timothy 3:1-9; 2 Peter 2:12-15).

And it is at this time that New Jerusalem comes down out of Heaven to land on the new earth, and then the marriage of the Lamb takes place (Revelation 21:2-6).

And New Jerusalem is where Jesus lives with his Bride for all of eternity (Song of Solomon 1:4c).

PART TWO

Getting to Know Our Neighbors – The Israelites

CHAPTER ONE
Psalm Six Analyzed[11]

I. Introduction:

I decided to analyze this Psalm because I find it amazing how thorough the repentance of the Old Testament Israelite was (i.e. Daniel 9:4-19).

II. Parallel and like Psalms:

Psalm 38, Psalm 39, Psalm 51 and Psalm 88 were somewhat parallel to this Psalm.

III. Theme, message, or title:

Often, we experience hardship from other people, and it is because these people are living for Satan (John 8:44). And since certain people are living for Satan,

---

[11] This theme paper was written to fulfill requirements for the course entitled, "Intro to Psalms" (B-An 601), at Faith Baptist Bible College and Seminary, Ankeny, IA. during the fall semester of 1976.

they can be tools for him. This is what King David experienced, and these people became his enemies.

Since this psalm was written by King David at a time when he was being chastened for sin, a title could be: "A Psalm About the Chastened Child of God's Feelings and Yearnings Caused by His Enemies, and the Victory Gained Through Peace with God." Or, an alternate title could be, "Satanic Oppressions in the Life of the Believer and His Victory Over Them."

IV. The Text:

Psalm six reads as follows:[12]

[1] To the chief music-maker on corded instruments, on the Sheminith. A Psalm of David. O Lord, do not be bitter with me in your wrath; do not send punishment on me in the heat of your passion. [2] Have mercy on me, O Lord, for I am wasted away: make me well, for even my bones are troubled. [3] My soul is in bitter trouble; and you, O Lord, how long? [4] Come back, O Lord, make my soul free; O give me salvation because of your mercy. [5] For in death there is no memory of you; in the grave who will give you praise? [6] The voice of my sorrow is a weariness to me; all the night I make my bed wet with weeping; it is watered by the drops flowing from my eyes. [7] My eyes are wasting away with trouble; they are becoming old because of all those who are against me. [8] Go from me, all you workers of evil; for the Lord has given ear to the voice of my weeping. [9] The Lord

---

[12] BBE version (Bible in Basic English) by Professor S. H. Hooke. Copyrighted in the United States of America by E.P. Dutton & Co., New York – 1941, and by Cambridge Press, Edinburg - 1965.

has given ear to my request; the Lord has let my prayer come before him. [10] Let all those who are against me be shamed and deeply troubled; let them be turned back and suddenly put to shame.

V. New Testament Reconciliation:

Before we begin, we must take into account the fact that there are in this Psalm certain theological statements that are hard to reconcile with New Testament theology. For instance, in verse five there is a vague reference to a lack of faith in eternal life. How is this to be reconciled with John 3:16? As also there is the question of an imprecation such as is found in verse ten.

The above problems, however, are not too hard to understand if progressive revelation is taken into account. For instance, Keil and Delitzsch have this to say,

> The Old Testament barrier encompasses the germinating New Testament life which at a future time shall burst it. The eschatology of the Old Testament leaves a dark background, which as is designed, is divided by the New Testament revelation into light and darkness, and is to be illumined into a wide perspective extending into the eternity beyond time. Everywhere, where it begins to dawn in this eschatological darkness of the Old Testament, it is the first morning rays of the New Testament sunrise which is

already announcing itself. The Christian also, here, cannot refrain from leaping the barrier of the Psalmist, and understand the Psalms according to the mind of the Spirit...[13]

So also this Psalm has an application to the persecuted Christian to show him he is fighting a spiritual battle against his enemies.[14] The resultant show of faith at the end of the Psalm, however, is to show that the Christian can overcome these feelings by exercising those things which are at his command, namely "Christ in him" or "the mind of Christ."

As F. W. Cobb says,

But I feel there are other sources than men that are the psalmist's enemies - namely Satan and his host. This is in accord with what Job experienced. However, I feel that Job's was not so much a chastening due to judgment, but one out of God's loving kindness in the growth of His child. On the other hand, the chastening in Psalm 6 is direct punishment by yielding to Satan, (John 12:26; Rom. 6:16).[15]

---

[13] C. F. Keil and F. Delitzsch (translated from German by James Martin*), Commentary on the Old Testament in Ten Volumes, vol. v, Psalms,* (William B. Eerdmans Publishing Company, Grand Rapids, MI - 1867), pp 77, 78.

[14] This is to say that it is actually spiritual "principalities" that David is fighting against (Ephesians 6:12).

[15] W. F. Cobb, D. D., *The Book of Psalms,* (Methuen and Co., W. C., London - 1905) p. 12.

The chastening has also inflicted all three parts of David's being, body, soul and spirit and is, indeed, thorough and heavy. Why this was brought upon the Lord's servant is probably because of his sin with Bathsheba. So not only is his conscience buffeting him, but also God's chastening through spiritual buffeting.

VI. The Text Examined (as far as David's chastening is concerned):

A. We will interpret verses 1b to 7 as strophes, verses 8-10 being antistrophic.

> 1. Strophe Number One (v.1b,c): In deep distress David cries to God.
> > [1b]. . . O Lord, do not be bitter with me in your wrath; do not send punishment on me in the heat of your passion.[16]

> 2. Strophe Number Two (vs.2, 3):
> > [2] Have mercy on me, O Lord, for I am wasted away: make me well, for even my bones are troubled. [3] My soul is in bitter trouble; and you, O Lord, how long?[17]
> > > a. David prays to God to let him experience mercy instead of the chastening of which he is undergoing. (v. 2a,b)

---

[16] BBE version (Bible in Basic English), op. cit.
[17] Ibid.

b. David also tells God that all three parts of his tri-partite being are affected by this chastening.

c. The distresses greatly affect his body in verse two, and his soul and spirit are affected in verse three.

    i. He is almost void of physical strength (v. 2c).

    ii. He is inflicted deep within his soul(v. 3a).

    iii. He doesn't have much spiritual strength (v. 3b).

3. Strophe Number Three (vs. 4, 5): The result of David's spiritual lapse of faith:
    [4] Come back, O Lord, make my soul free; O give me salvation because of your mercy. [5] For in death there is no memory of you; in the grave who will give you praise?[18]

These two verses seem to be telling of David's lack of faith in eternal life, and it is true the Israelites had only a nominal knowledge of it.

However, we will examine how the ancient Israelites viewed eternal life in the next chapter of this book.

---

[18] Ibid.

4. strophe number four (v. 6a):

6a The voice of my sorrow is a weariness to me; [19]

This strophe depicts the fact that David is tired of repenting, because when there is deep repentance, it is hard to do, both spiritually and physically.

5. Strophe number five (v. 6b,c):

6b,c all the night I make my bed wet with weeping; it is watered by the drops flowing from my eyes. [20]

This strophe is depicted by the fact that David's soul is hurting so much it is making him break out in tears (6b,c):

6. Strophe Number Six (v.7a): David cannot think clearly:

7a My eyes are wasting away with trouble; [21]

This strophe is depicted by David's inability to grasp reality due to spiritual darkness.

7. Strophe Number Seven (v. 7b): David is in the depths of his grief:

7b they are becoming old because of all those who are against me. [22]

---

[19] Ibid.

[20] Ibid.

[21] Ibid.

[22] Ibid.

David has the perception that he is growing old prematurely because of this chastening. And he knows it is because of the contrariness of his enemies.

B. David Gaines Victory Through Faith (vs. 8, 9)

[8] Go from me, all you workers of evil; for the Lord has given ear to the voice of my weeping. [9] The Lord has given ear to my request; the Lord has let my prayer come before him.[23]

David shows faith by acknowledging that God has heard his prayer.

C. David Comes to a Place of Victory: The victory is in the form of an imprecation (v. 10):

[10] Let all those who are against me be shamed and deeply troubled; let them be turned back and suddenly put to shame.[24]

1. Because the faith that David is displaying is being manifested in the form of an imprecation, it brings us to the question as to whether imprecations are relevant and necessary for us today in the Church dispensation.

---

[23] Ibid.
[24] Ibid.

Keil and Delitzsch throw some light on this with the following:

> We have come to examine the relation of the Psalms to the New Testament righteousness of faith and to the New Testament morality which flows from the primary command of infinite love. Both with respect to the atonement and to redemption, the Psalms undergo a complete metamorphosis in the consciousness of the praying New Testament church - a metamorphosis, rendered possible by the unveiling and particularizing of salvation that has since taken place.
>
> So in the position occupied by the Christian and by the church towards the enemies of Christ, the desire for their removal is certainly outweighed by the desire for their conversion: but assuming, that they will not be converted and will not anticipate their punishment, the transition from a feeling of love to that of wrath is warranted in the New Testament (e. g. Galatians 5:12), and assuming their absolute Satanic hardness of heart, the Christian even may not shrink from praying for their final overthrow. For the kingdom of God comes not only by the way of mercy but also of judgment; and the coming of the kingdom of God is the goal of the Old as

well as of the New Testament saint, and every wish that judgment may descend upon those who oppose the coming of the kingdom of God is cherished even in the Psalms on the assumption of their lasting impenitence.[25]

2. Prayer, not Vengeance:

Mr. Clarence Benson, a contemporary, evangelical scholar, tells us that imprecations are warranted in the New Testament Church, and that they should be in the form of a prayer.

Mr. Benson says,

When the Psalmist called upon God to take vengeance on the wicked, was he not anticipating the teaching of the New Testament? Vengeance belongs to God, He will repay (Romans 12:19).

Instead of taking vengeance into his own hands, David was asking his righteous God to judge iniquity.

There is certainly nothing wrong in praying for God to break the teeth of wicked men who are using those teeth to tear the upright.

The language of the Hebrew people is direct and concrete, not abstract. Where we speak of crime, they designate the

---

[25] C. F. Keil and F. Delitzsch, op. cit., pp 72 and 74.

criminal. The Christian, on the other hand is taught to have compassion on the sinner, but to abhor his sin. [26]

VII. Conclusion:

It is evident that we must make a transition from the fear that is found in verses one to seven to the victory that is found in verses eight to ten. And we have seen that to be out of fellowship with God is not a good place to be. Psalm Six attests to that.

So, this Psalm shows an awesome repentance and the resultant show of faith.

[26] Clarence H. Benson, Litt. D., *Unit II, Old Testament Survey, Poetry, and Prophecy,* (Evangelical Teacher Training Association, Wheaton, IL. - 1963) pp 20-21.

CHAPTER TWO

Life, Death, Eternal Life, and the Ancient Hebrew[27]

There is a question after a thorough study of the Psalms that I feel warrants consideration at this time. That is, why do sometimes the ancient Hebrews think of death in terms of personal loss? Such passages as Psalms 6:5; 30:9: 88:10; and 89:48 suggest this, even though Psalms 30:11,12; 16:10; and 17:15 seem to say they can at times believe in eternal life.

Let us look at three aspects of this that will give insight into the matter. They are: 1.) life here on earth; 2.) death; and 3.) eternal life.

---

[27] This treatise was also written to fulfill requirements for the class entitled, Psalms (B-An 601) at Faith Baptist Bible College and Seminary, Ankeny, Iowa during the fall semester of 1976.

I. Life and the Israelite:

Mr. H. C. Leupold says that, "praise of the Creator was an important part of the life of God's people,"[28] so it was very important that they be allowed to do it.

In fact, giving God praise was to the Israelite commensurate with life itself, because they thought if it were to be lacking in their lives, they were out of fellowship with Him, and being out of fellowship with God meant that they were not experiencing life to its fullest. This is why Mr. L. Swain says that,

> For the Hebrew mind, human life is such
> an absolute and positive value, it would
> be superfluous for the Hebrew to qualify
> what he knew to be human life in its
> fullness with the epithet."[29]

In other words, to be alive was to praise God, and to be in a place where you could not praise God, was disastrous. This is why if it could not be done, it was equivalent to being near to death, a sorrowful position to be in for sure.

This being the case, not being able to praise God was also equated with a loss of eternal standing with God, and is why Mr. and Mrs. Briggs while commenting on Psalms 88:4 say that,

---

[28] H. C. Leupold, *Exposition of the Psalms*, (Baker Book House, Grand, Rapids, MI - 1969), p. 630.

[29] L. Swain, *Clergy Review*, (Baker Book House, Grand Rapids, MI - 1967), p. 105.

> Misfortunes and calamities have come
> upon them in such numbers, and to
> so great an extent, that they have had
> more than enough, more than they are
> able to endure. [30]

This, then, would signify that when an Israelite found himself in a position of persecution, he became very discouraged. In view of this, the positive attitude of the ancient Hebrew that was usually manifested through praise was gone, and he felt he no longer had true life.

II. Death, and the Israelite:

Mr. and Mrs. Briggs, while commenting on Psalms 88:3b-6 tell us that the passages that speak of going down to the pit are speaking of the thoughts and feelings of one who is experiencing spiritual death, or in New Testament language, one who has been put into a castaway position (I Cor. 5:5; 9:27). They say,

> . . . 'my life has arrived' [meaning
> they have] made the journey toward it
> and actually arrived there. [Likewise],
> 'them that go down to the pit' [meaning
> they were] descending in death to the
> abode of the dead and going still further
> down into the pit, in Sheol, the abode

---

[30] Charles Augustus Briggs and Emlie Grace Briggs,_*The International Critical Commentary*, the section entitled: "A Critical and Exegetical Commentary on the Book of Psalms, Vol. II.", (T. & T. Clark, Edinburgh - 1969), p. 244.

of the wretched dead, cf. 28:1; 30:4; 143:7. They were already 'counted', or enumerated among such, as if they were among the dead. [31]

This, then, says that if you have fallen into sin and are out of fellowship with God, you are experiencing a lower form of life, or one that is commensurate with Sheol or death.

III. Eternal Life and the Israelite:

It is a given fact that the ancient Israelite believed that what you did here in this life was merit or demerit for the future. Couple this with the fact that they did not believe in going to Heaven when they died, and you have a depressing attitude toward dying.

Leupold has said,

Only on this level of enlightenment could men of the Old Testament pray thus, 'What profit is there in my blood if I go down to the pit?' when the truth concerning the resurrection of the body was not yet fully revealed or grasped, and the glorious life in the hereafter was not sufficiently understood.[32]

I think this is an answer to the problem. Because of the resurrection of our Lord and Savior, Jesus Christ, who is the "first-fruits," (meaning He was the first person

---

[31] Ibid.

[32] Leupold, op. cit., p. 255.

to be resurrected to eternal life), He was able to give eternal life to all who believe. And this had not been revealed to the ancient Hebrew yet, so, the resurrection of the Israelite's body in the future was not understood. Granted, Job in chapter 42, verse 5 speaks of a time in which he said he would "see God" after the death of his body, but the time, place, and method were not fully revealed. It is true that before the cross, the Hebrew people were looking for a savior, but he was in the form of a king to sit on David's throne, not one who would promise them eternal life in Heaven with Him.

So, the ancient Hebrew did not understand that they must ultimately receive new bodies to live in the future. What happened after death to them was a mystery, because they were looking at the Abrahamic Covenant (Genesis 12) and seeing that they would be large in numbers and inheriting the land that they were living on forever. They did not grasp the fact that they would be going to Heaven someday.

CHAPTER THREE

Israel During the Great Tribulation

After rejecting their savior, Jesus Christ, and after almost two thousand years of trouble, the rapture of the Church comes about, and the nation of Israel is left behind to go through the great tribulation. During that time, they accept an imposter (Daniel 9:25-27) who is the anti-Christ. They make a peace-pact with him and he ultimately occupies their land.

The occupation of Israel is seen in Daniel 8:11-12, as well as in Daniel 11:41 and 45. This happens in the middle of the tribulation period (Daniel 9:27; Revelation12:6), after the anti-Christ betrays them. But those Israelites who find God's favor will be hidden "in the wilderness" (Daniel 12:1c,d; Revelation 12:6,14), and when the great tribulation is over they will go into the Millennium.

In regard to the anti-Christ occupying the land of Israel, Daniel 8:11-12 says,

> [11] It [the anti-Christ] set itself up to be as great as the commander of the army of the LORD; it took away the daily sacrifice from the LORD, and his sanctuary was thrown down. [12] Because of rebellion, the LORD's people and the daily sacrifice were given over to it. It prospered in everything it did, and truth was thrown to the ground. [33]

As also Daniel 11:41 says,

> He will also invade the Beautiful Land. Many countries will fall, but Edom, Moab and the leaders of Ammon will be delivered from his hand.[34]

It's interesting that "Edom, Moab and the leaders of Ammon" will be delivered from his hand. This, I believe, is where the righteous people living in Israel during the Tribulation will be hidden out! These three countries are where the country of Jordan is today.

And finally, Daniel 11:45 says,

> He will pitch his royal tents between the seas at the beautiful holy mountain. Yet he will come to his end, and no one will help him.[35]

---

[33] New International Version of the Bible, (B. B. Kirkbride Bible Co., Inc., - Indianapolis, IN; Zondervan Bible Publishers – Grand Rapids, MI.)

[34] Ibid.

[35] Ibid.

However, aren't you glad that the second chance for the Hebrew people comes about as the Millennium? This is the one thousand years that Israel will have their king, Jesus Christ, sitting on David's throne in Jerusalem, after which she will finally be made ready to be married to Jesus when the Millennium has been completed!

In outline form, the events that affect the nation of Israel during the great tribulation are as follows:

I. The Anti-Christ is Revealed:

The first things that happens, and this is right after rapture of the Church, the great tribulation starts, and the anti-Christ is revealed. This is seen in 2 Thessalonians 2:7-9 which reads as follows in the NIV,

> [7] For the secret power of lawlessness is already at work; but the one who now holds it back will continue to do so till he is taken out of the way. [8] And then the lawless one will be revealed, whom the Lord Jesus will overthrow with the breath of his mouth and destroy by the splendor of his coming. [9] The coming of the lawless one will be in accordance with how Satan works. He will use all sorts of displays of power through signs and wonders that serve the lie. . .

So it can be seen that right after the rapture of the Church the anti-Christ is revealed, the 'holding back' in verse seven being the indwelling of the Holy Spirit in Christians.

The anti-Christ is also depicted in Daniel 11:21 as someone who comes into power by intrigue, and in verse 23 as someone who has a small oligarchy at his command.

This is because everything that is said before verse 36 of Daniel, chapter 11 is historical in nature, describing people like Antiochus Epiphanies IV. He is a type of the anti-Christ, because he also desecrated the temple at Jerusalem.[36]

However, beginning with verse 36 it switches to the eschatological future, because this is the first time the term "king" is given to an individual in this passage without it being either the king of the north or the king of the south. This does not mean, however, that other despotic rulers that are found prior to verse 36 cannot also be types of the anti-Christ.

II. The Peace Treaty Made with Israel by the anti-Christ:

Daniel 9:27 tells of a "covenant" (and I think this covenant is a peace treaty between Israel and the anti-Christ's regime) that is made between Israel and the

---

[36] In the book of Daniel, chapters 8- 11, there are both 'near prophecies' and 'far prophecies'' in the same passage of scripture. A near prophesy is fulfilled by history not too far from when it was given, but a far prophesy must wait for the eschatological future to be fulfilled.

See the writings of Bill Lee-Warner (Grace Sola Foundation, Inc.) where he speaks of the "near future" which is Antiochus Epiphones IV, and the "far future" which is the anti-Christ.

anti-Christ, with the leader of Israel being called "the prince of the covenant" in Daniel 11:22.

III. The Covenant Abolished by the Abomination of Desolation:

The covenant that has been made between Israel and the anti-Christ is broken in the middle of the tribulation period (Daniel 9:27; Revelation 12:6)[37] by the abomination of desolation. This act by Antiochus Epiphanies IV is where he sacrifices a pig on the alter in the temple in Jerusalem. But it is also when the anti-Christ sets up an image of himself in the 3rd Temple in Jerusalem that will be built in the future. He then takes the daily sacrifices away (Daniel 8:11-12).

IV. Armageddon Happens:

The battle of Armageddon is when the world's armies gathers around Jerusalem to finally and for all time try to do away with Israel. It is found in Daniel 11:45b; Zechariah 14:2-5; Zechariah 12:11; Revelation 12:13-16; Revelation 16:16 and Revelation 19:11-21.

Walvoord says while commenting on Revelation 16:16 that,

> The armies of the world contending for honors on the battlefield at the very time of the second coming of Christ do all turn, however, and combine their efforts against Christ

---

[37] Weeks in eschatology are actually years.

and His army from heaven when the glory of the second coming appears in the heavens"[38]

V. The Glorious Second Coming of Jesus Christ:

When Jesus Christ comes back the second time (Rev. 19:11-21), all He has to do is start speaking and that war called Armageddon crumbles. It is at this time that the anti-Christ and the false prophet are captured and put directly into the lake of fire, and everybody else is killed by the words that Jesus is saying (Revelation 19:20,21).

That the judgment of the anti-Christ and false-Prophet happens very quickly tells us that it is not a very wise thing to fight against Jesus Christ. And it is also not expedient to persecute the nation of Israel of which the battle of Armageddon started out to be.

There are many places in the Book of Revelation that say Jesus will "come quickly" (Revelation 2:16; 3:11; 11:14; 22:7, 12, and 20). He proves this at the end of the tribulation period.

So now the world is ready for the Millennium to start, because of these events.

---

[38] Walvoord, op. cit., p. 237.

EPILOGUE

In the last few weeks of finishing this book, October 7, 2023 happened. On that terrible day Hamas snuck out of their tunnels from the Gaza strip and terrorized and murdered a lot of Israelites who lived nearby.

A friend of mine said of this that "the Lord will not let the devil destroy Israel!'

This is true, Jesus Christ has always had strategic plans concerning Israel, because they were a witness to the Gentiles since their conception, they brought forth Jesus Christ through the virgin Mary and, lastly, most of the New Testament was written through Jewish men who became Jesus' apostles.

But right now, the stage is being set for a bright future for the nation of Israel, because they will be going into their future Millennium where they have a second chance to live for Jesus Christ.

I like Revelation, chapter twelve because it portrays a running history leading up to the Jewish nation's path toward the Millennium. It reads as follows in the new International Version,

> [1] A great sign appeared in heaven: a woman clothed with the sun, with the

moon under her feet and a crown of twelve stars on her head. [2] She was pregnant and cried out in pain as she was about to give birth. [3] Then another sign appeared in heaven: an enormous red dragon with seven heads and ten horns and seven crowns on its heads. [4] Its tail swept a third of the stars out of the sky and flung them to the earth. The dragon stood in front of the woman who was about to give birth, so that it might devour her child the moment he was born. [5] She gave birth to a son, a male child, who "will rule all the nations with an iron scepter." And her child was snatched up to God and to his throne. [6] The woman fled into the wilderness to a place prepared for her by God, where she might be taken care of for 1,260 days.

[7] Then war broke out in heaven. Michael and his angels fought against the dragon, and the dragon and his angels fought back. [8] But he was not strong enough, and they lost their place in heaven. [9] The great dragon was hurled down—that ancient serpent called the devil, or Satan, who leads the whole world astray. He was hurled to the earth, and his angels with him.

[10] Then I heard a loud voice in heaven say:

"Now have come the salvation and the power and the kingdom of our God,
and the authority of his Messiah.

For the accuser of our brothers and sisters,

who accuses them before our God, day and night, has been hurled down.

[11] They triumphed over him by the blood of the Lamb and by the word of their testimony;

they did not love their lives so much as to shrink from death.

[12] Therefore rejoice, you heavens and you who dwell in them!

But woe to the earth and the sea, because the devil has gone down to you!

He is filled with fury, because he knows that his time is short."

[13] When the dragon saw that he had been hurled to the earth, he pursued the woman who had given birth to the male child. [14] The woman was given the two wings of a great eagle, so that she might fly to the place prepared for her in the wilderness, where she would be taken care of for a time, times and half a time, out of the serpent's reach. [15] Then from his mouth the serpent spewed water like a river, to overtake the woman and sweep her away with the torrent. [16] But the earth helped the woman by opening its mouth and swallowing the river that the dragon had spewed out of his

> mouth. [17] Then the dragon was enraged at the woman and went off to wage war against the rest of her offspring—those who keep God's commands and hold fast their testimony about Jesus.[39]

Isn't this chapter of the Bible fascinating? It gives the history of the 1st coming of Jesus Christ (v. 5), tells of the ascension of Jesus to sit on a throne next to God the Father (5b), tells of the loss of Satan's place in heaven (vs. 7-13), tells of the protection of the nation of Israel during the second half of the tribulation period (vs. 6,14), tells of Satan's behavior during the Great Tribulation (vs. 13-16) and ends with the wrath that Satan will build up during his incarceration for a thousand years (v.17). This last item really shows his stubbornness in that he will not give up, and even thinks he can still do away with Israel at the end of the Millennium (Revelation 20:1-3; 7-10). But fire comes out of Heaven and devours everyone who will take part in this final rebellion (Revelation 20:7-10).

---

[39] New International Version of the Bible, op. cit.

SECTION THREE
Two Short Stories

A Community Church for Eastern Long Island

by
Jeremy Johnson

A new church was created when my family became involved in building a local church in a village of eastern Long Island, New York. We moved there because my grandfather saw an article on the internet about how there was a village in eastern Long Island that had no churches, and he decided to do something about it!

It was soon after that he found an awesome house for sale with a huge 'great room', and he felt it would make an excellent 'starter church building'. He also realized his family could all live in this house, and he and Dad could commute to work in Manhattan from the airport near the village!

So, we all became home missionaries by starting a New Testament church on Long Island!

Hi, my name is Jeremy Johnson, and I now live on Long Island with my grandparents, parents and my twin sister!

My grandfather's name is Joshua Johnson the 2nd, however, Dad's name is Jerrod Johnson. My mother's name is Megan, my grandmother's is Susan, and

Jennifer is my sister's name. We are all born again Christians!

My grandparents live in the mother-in-law section of the house and my parents have the upstairs master suite. I have the suite above Joshua and Susan's suite, and Jennifer has the other suite at the other side of the house.

The great room is truly a great room because the ceiling is $2\frac{1}{2}$ stories high, and that's why we bought the house; it looks like a church.

The great room is between the two ends of the house where the bedrooms are. However, below my parents' (and sisters') bedrooms is the kitchen, pantry and dining nook.

Our cook, Sarah, is an excellent one, and she and her husband, John, who is the gardener, live in the newly built basement. It's newly built because the basement was nicely finished when we bought the house, but it didn't have any walls put in. But now it has a nice apartment down there!

We have at least 30 people who come every Sunday to our church, which include John and Sarah. We were acquainted with them in Manhattan because they attended the downtown church that we attended.

Grandpa and Grandma, as well as John and Sarah, hold down everything during the week when my parents are in NYC working.

Jenny and I go to a high school nearby where I met, Kelly, my sweetheart!

The property Next Door:

Our church had grown to about 50 people, so parking had become a problem. The property just west of ours between Main Street and our house became for sale just in time. We were able to buy it and put a parking lot behind the big old house there.

Also, we changed the driveway to the main house from the cold black top that it was to cement and made it two lanes wide. You can now access the new parking lot from that driveway.

There is also a wide sidewalk going from the parking lot across this driveway to the front door of the main house. The flagstone sidewalk to the front door of the main house was taken out when the two-lane driveway was put in and a circular cement drive was put in front instead. This helps with the safety of our church members. John takes the husbands to the front door from the parking lot in the large SUV that was purchased for that purpose!

You are probably wondering where all the money for all this comes from. The fact that my family is debt free is because Great-grandfather, Joshua, started a bank on Manhattan in New York City after the Great Depression and was good at investing on Wall Street! The bank was never very large and was bought out by a larger one, however, the investment part remains to this day and is owned by my family. It is lucrative, because we let Jesus do the decision making!

Two Years Later:

I decided to attend business school in NYC after high school. Kelly and I were married after we graduated, and then we moved to Manhattan, and Kelly attends art school there. She is very busy going to school during the week, and I take her there and pick her up in the afternoon.

I'm just glad that after business school, I was allowed to be a partner in the business, along with Dad. (Grandpa is retired now and stays in Long Island!)

Jenny is talented, because she has a contemporary Christian music voice. She is attending a Bible College in Cedarville, Ohio, where she hopes she can find a godly husband!

When I was in high school, I would sometimes work a week during the summer at the office in NYC. Our family has an apartment on Manhattan that has three bedrooms, and I occupied one of them.

Since Grandpa and Grandma are retired, they are happy living on Long Island. Grandpa is actually the pastor, and Grandma also does a lot of visitation along with him for the Long Island Community Church.

A New Church Building:

The church has been growing due to advertising on the internet, and we had to start planning a new church building! In fact, the next three properties that are south of the new parking lot became for sale. We negotiated for them and ended up buying them. It came about without a hitch, because the Lord was in it!

These four properties between our main house and Main Street will be ample room for the new church building after the four old houses on them are torn down.

Six Months Later:

Construction has started on the new church building and is coming along nicely!!!

One and a Half Years Later:

The new church building is finished now and there were no problems constructing it. We put the new church close to Main Street and extended the existing parking lot beside it and behind it. We are glad we had that other parking lot, because the new church sits on a rather narrow piece of land. However, since the educational wing is narrower than the sanctuary, it gives us more parking space beside the church, and there is vertical parking in front on Main Street.

The new church sits on the property so that the front door to the sanctuary, with a drive-through canopy, is at the back of the sanctuary giving traffic on Main Street in front of the church a view of the huge window at the front of the sanctuary. This window has a huge cross in it and is well lit at night for all to see!

We now have a lot of room for church-wide fellowship in the new fellowship hall in the basement of the new church. We also enjoy getting to know each other better down there when we have pot-luck dinners!

The Remodeling of the Basement in the main House:

When the new church was built, the Sunday school classrooms in the basement of the main house became two very large dorm-like bedrooms, and the two Sunday school bathrooms that were down there were each moved to the new bedrooms. These two dorms became the sleeping places for the children that come to our summer camp every year. It is not a large camp and usually ranges around 15 to 25 children. In the last few years they had slept in the old house in front of the new parking lot. It had two stories, so there was plenty of room for them.

John and Sarah's apartment is still in the basement of the main house, however, the two new bedrooms are right near the outside stairway from the basement which is very handy for the campers to get to the swimming pool in the back yard.

The poolhouse in front of the pool has always served as a church piocnic food layout place, but it now has an added function; there is a kareoki machine in the downstairs of the poolhouse. In other words, the poolhouse is the recreation center for the camp, but Classes are held in the new church building which isn't that far away!

When Jenny and Her Husband Come to Visit:

Jenny was successful at finding a husband at Cedarville College; his name is Brian. He became a pastor in Iowa after they graduated, and when they come to visit in the summer they act as camp counselors. Kelly and I love to be camp counselors, also.

My Family's week-ends

Since Joshua and Susan are retired from the family business, they bought a house next door to the church which is south of the sanctuary. Grandpa has an office in the church, because, after all, he is the pastor!

He, Dad and John have always done the preaching on Sunday mornings, and I also take my turn every fourth Sunday now.

Kelly and I stay in the nice guest suite at Kelly's parents' house every weekend, and we ride to church with them! John delivers Kelly and I to her parents' house from the airport on Saturday as he delivers my parents to the main house where they stay in their former suite upstairs. John and Sarah have moved to Grandpa and Grandma's former suite on the main floor, and their former apartment in the basement is the guest suite where guest speakers stay.

Ten Years Later:

The church is doing well. We have people who come from as far away as New York City and beyond, as well as those who live in our village. We are a loving independent church which has no problems as far as everyone getting along with each other. Praise The Lord!!!!

What We Believe:

OUR BASIS OF FAITH at Long Island Community Church:

The truths about God and His creation are revealed in the Bible. It is such a wonderful book because it is the Word of God. Because of this, we believe in:

1. The only true God who lives eternally in three persons: The Father, The Son and The Holy Spirit.

2. The love, grace and sovereignty of God in creating, sustaining, ruling, redeeming and judging the world.

3. The divine inspiration and supreme authority of the Old and New Testament scriptures, which are the written Word of God! They are fully trustworthy for faith and conduct.

4. The dignity of all people, male and female, created in God's image to love others, be holy and care for creation, yet corrupted by sin, which means they must be redeemed.

5. The incarnation of God's eternal Son, the Lord Jesus Christ, who was born of the virgin Mary, was truly divine and truly human, yet without sin.

6. The atoning sacrifice of Jesus Christ on the cross, dying in our place, paying the price for our sins and defeating evil. In doing so, He reconciled us with God if we believe in Him.

7. The bodily resurrection of Jesus Christ, His ascension to the Father and his reign and mediation as the only Savior of the world.

8. The justification of sinners solely by the grace of God through faith in Jesus Christ.

9. The ministry of God the Holy Spirit, who leads us to repentance, teaches us God's truth from the Bible, unites us with Christ through the new birth, empowers our discipleship and enables our witness for bringing the lost to Christ.

The Holy Spirit also teaches us what the apostles taught, apostles such as John, Paul and Peter who advocated the doctrine of sanctification, especially when the apostle Paul said in Romans, chapter six to determine something to be sin and then to just not do it! He also pointed out in verse four of chapter six of the book of Romans that, "like as Christ was raised up from the dead by the glory of the Father, even so we also should walk in newness of life."

We also believe every born-again believer is endowed with the Holy Spirit's 21 spiritual gifts. Each person has at least one of them for the purpose of worshiping God and proclaiming the "whole counsel of God".

10. The Church, the body of Christ both local and Universal. We also believe in the priesthood of all believers who are given new life by the Holy Spirit to promote justice and love.
11. The coming of Jesus Christ in the clouds to rapture all born-again believers up to Heaven to be with Him. This is known as The Rapture of the Church (1 Thessalonians 4:13-18; Revelation 3:10). After this event, He will give His saints a marriage supper of the Lamb of which afterwards He will give rewards at the Judgement Seat of Christ.

We also believe in the Second Coming of Christ to curtail the persecution of Israel and to bring them into 1000 years of having Jesus Christ as their king, sitting on David's throne in Jerusalem.

After the Millennium and after the Great white throne Judgment, the latter of which all unsaved people will be at, Jesus Christ creates a new heaven and new earth where He will live in New Jerusalem with His new bride for all of eternity.

A Colorado House and Home

by
Jake Weiss

The House:

The house I live in has four wings and looks like a plus sign from the air. But two of the wings are shorter than the other two and are the dining room at the rear of the house and the great room at the front.

Outside the dining room, which has a huge window almost the size of the wall on the west side of it, is the backyard (however, there is no swimming pool).

The dining room and backyard are actually one story lower than the three wings upstairs, because the house is built on the side of a hill.

There is a two-bedroom suite on the 2nd floor of the bedroom wing, the bedrooms having ensuite bathrooms.

This suite has a living room with a couple of leather recliners for watching TV when not studying. It also has two study desks in this living room, and the suite has a kitchenette with a small refrigerator and a microwave oven. There is also a double sink with a small dish cabinet above it. This suite is where my little brother, Brian, and I sleep.

There is a two-bedroom suite on the 1st floor of this bedroom wing that also has a living room and kitchenette. It is where my two sisters, Jenny and Chloe sleep.

The layout of the bedroom suite on the first floor is exactly like the one om the 2nd, and these two suites are set up for people who go to school like my siblings and I do!

Beside the kitchenette in both of these suites is the square arch for entering the bedroom hall that has five somewhat narrow, perpendicular windows in it.

In the living room of each suite there is a sliding glass door that goes out to a balcony, however, the balcony does not extend to the bedrooms, so it is not that big.

At the end of the hallway in each of these suites is a door that the 2nd floor one goes out to a stairway in an enclosed staircase which has a two-story window in it. The staircase only goes down one floor, because on the 1st floor a stairway is not necessary, due to the fact that Jenny and Chloe's suite is at the front lawn level.

When you come out that door from the hallway on the 2nd floor, you will find a landing, and from this landing you must take a right turn to go down that stairway. The stairway has a glass side on the left of it with a wood railing above the glass. On the right side of the stairway along the wall there is a wood railing that matches the one on the other side. At the 1st floor level there is a vestibule with a door going outside.

The door at the end of the hallway of Jenny and Chloe's bedroom suite goes out to be under the stairway coming from upstairs and you go between it and the outside wall to get to the door going outside from the vestibule. Beyond the door going outside (because the door going outside faces south and the stairway descends to the west) there is room for a bicycle rack that can hold six bicycles.

Our house sits on 75 acres out in the woods, and you come down a long lane from the street that goes to the right of the great room in front of the house. It then goes to the seven-car garage on the north side of the house, so this garage and the great room comprise the other two wings. This means, we have the bedroom wing, the garage wing, the great room wing and the dining room wing.

At the back of the property there is a good-sized valley with a very small creek running through it, and the far edge of the backyard hangs over that valley.

There are two small patios, as well as, a large one outside the dining room. The large one is on the south side of the dining room, and also there is a narrow patio in front of the dining room window. And there is a small patio on the north side of the dining room.

In the south patio there is an outside kitchen, and we love having picnics out there. Beyond the patios is a lawn that has a wrought iron fence on top of a brick wall all around it.

The dining room has a ceramic tile floor and is where there is also, of course, the kitchen.

The furnace room is directly behind the kitchen and the game/exercise room is directly behind the furnace room.

The kitchen has a serving bar that divides it from the dining room, this serving bar seating seven people, and it is reminiscent of an old-time soda fountain! There is also a huge dining table in the middle of the dining room where there is room for over 20 people to sit down during a meal!

These are all beneath the family/living room (great room) that is at the front of the house. This great room has many couches for which to sit on and have Bible studies!!

There is a large foyer behind the great room that has ceramic tile on the floor, also! This foyer has two wings on each end of it, one is the bedroom wing that was described earlier, and the other wing is the seven-car garage. The seven-car garage has Sarah, the maid and, Johnny the caretaker's, apartment above it. Under the garage is a one-bedroom apartment where Johnny used to live. He is married to Sarah and they are a sweet black couple who met after they were hired by us!

Johnny's former apartment has only one bedroom, and there is the north half of the backyard in front of it. The dumpster driveway comes into the backyard back there, and along with a flower garden they make the north patio much smaller than the south one. The patio that is in front of the dining room window is just a narrow sliver to get you from one patio to the other.

There is also a two-bedroom apartment that is at the backyard level below Jenny and Chloe's bedroom suite. This apartment is where Grandpa and Grandma Weiss live and has a front door going out into the hallway that goes to the game/exercise room.

The furnace room door is in this hallway, the furnace actually being a boiler and heats every radiator in every room of the house with steam heat.

And the bedrooms, as well as the living room, in Grandpa and Grandma's apartment have patio doors leading to the south patio that is outside this apartment.

The living room of Grandpa and Grandma's apartment also has a kitchenette with a serving bar dividing it from the living room. The serving bar seats five people, and you go beside the kitchenet to access the hallway to the bedrooms just like the two floors above. The hallway has five small basement windows that are below the tall windows above them.

The two patios that are in front of the two apartments down there are accessible from two glass doors, one on each side of the dining room, due to the fact the dining room sticks out from the back of the house about 30 feet.

The north patio, dumpster driveway and flower garden are easily accessible from the north outside door of the dining room, as also the door that is on the other side of the dining room goes out to the south patio. There are outdoor tables and chairs in the south patio, as well as chaise lounges for getting a suntan on.

The front door of Jonny's former apartment goes out to the dining room from a hall coming from the living room, the hall being necessary because of the laundry room that takes square footage out of the apartment. Beside the door going into the dining room of this hall coming from the living room in Jonny's former apartment, there is a door going outside to a sidewalk beside the flower garden and it goes to the north dining room door, as well as the small a patio between the dumpster driveway and lawn.

The living room of Johnny's former apartment also has a kitchenette just like Grandpa and Grandma's, however, there are no sliding glass doors in both the living room and the bedroom. But there are good-sized windows instead.

And unlike Grandma and Grandpa's apartment, which has a long hallway, Johnny's former apartment only has a short hallway going to the one bedroom. This short hall is necessary because the bathroom is between the kitchenette and the bedroom.

There is a one-car garage at the north end of Johnny's former apartment that has the huge riding lawnmower in it, as well as the Bobcat that Johnny uses to take 110-gallon bags of garbage to the dumpster that is up north in a grove of trees. (There is also a special lawnmower that can mow the side of a bluff in the one-car garage!)

The dumpster driveway is connected to the driveway that comes from the parking lot in front of the seven-car garage. This creates a T-intersection up toward the north grove of trees where the dumpster is! (A heater cab is put on the Bobcat in the winter so Johnny will be toasty while taking the garbage out.)

There is a 500-gallon gas tank above the door to this one-car garage, the gas tank being for gassing up the lawnmowers, as well as the Bobcat, and a tanker truck comes and fills it up every once in a while.

You cannot get a suntan out on the north pool patio, because it is too narrow to have a lot of chaise lounges on. This is due to the flower garden and the dumpster driveway. So it only goes in a very narrow way along the east side of the lawn, and we love to play croquet on this lawn.

If you turn to the left after you go into the dining room from the north dining room door, you will see the hallway that leads to the laundry room as well as the north side of the kitchen. At the end of this hallway is the elevator that goes up to the great foyer behind the great room, as well as the master bedroom suite above the great room. Across that hallway from the laundry room is the swinging door leading into the kitchen, and inside the kitchen to the left is the door to the pantry. Food can be brought to the pantry and refrigerators in the kitchen from a vehicle that has backed down the dumpster driveway. It must back down, because there is no way for it to turn around down there without getting its front wheels on the patio which isn't good for the patio.

Food can also be brought down from a vehicle that has gone into the first parking space in the seven-car garage. Then when you do that, you must go out to the great foyer to access the elevator going down to the laundry room hallway. This is usually the way groceries are taken downstairs, though.

The master bedroom suite above the great room has a huge bathroom and two huge closets, one on each side of a very wide hallway that isn't a hallway at all, but is actually two dressing/closet areas that are accessed from an arch in the middle of the back of the huge master bedroom. So, you go through these two his-and-her dressing/closet sections to get to the door to the master bathroom.

The master bedroom, as well as the great room, each have two huge windows, one on the north and one on the south sides!

At the far end of the huge master bathroom there is a soaking tub and a big window. This window is two stories above the one in the dining room. And, of course, there is a double sink vanity with a very large glass enclosed shower across the room from the sinks.

There is a stairwell with a stairway in it at the east

end of the master bedroom and is for complying with fire regulations, as all of the stairways are. And the vestibule at the bottom of this stairwell is handy for keeping two bicycles in it!

When seen from the street, our house looks very symmetrical. The reason for this is that the garage wing is two stories high (from the lawn level) and has, Sarah and Johnny's apartment above it where Sarah and Johnny now live as newlyweds.

The south bedroom wing is the same way; it is two stories high at the front lawn level, and the hallways in the bedroom suites, as well as the apartment above the garage all have those five tall narrow perpendicular windows to add to the symmetrical effect.

There is also a staircase along the north side of the seven-car garage (with a tall window in it) that goes to Johnny and Sarah's apartment that also descends into a vestibule at the front lawn level. This vestibule has a door going into the garage and also a door going outside to the sidewalk coming from the huge parking area in front of the seven-car garage.

At the top of this stairwell going up to Sarah and Johnny's apartment, which has ceramic tile on the stairway and wood railings on both sides of it, there is a landing with the door to Johnny and Sarah's apartment, and you enter into a living room with a kitchenette just like Grandpa and Grandma's.

Going from the living room is the hall beside the two bedrooms, the bedrooms each having ensuite bathrooms. The living room of this apartment also has a sliding glass door to a small balcony just like in the south bedroom wing, making the back of the house look symmetrical, too.

I haven't mentioned the front door of the house yet; it goes into the great room near the 90-degree angle where the gage and great room meet and is a very ornate door. You come into the great room from it, and you can see most of the great foyer when you do that. This is due to the great arch at the back of the great room with four pillars in it.

At the south end of the great foyer there is a hallway going west down by the south bedroom wing. it goes to the T.V. room that is behind the powder room and coat closet that are for guests who come to visit. The doors of these two rooms are on the west side of the great foyer, and they are beside the stairway going to the dining room from up there.

There is also the door to Jenny and Chloe's bedrooms in the T.V. room hallway, as well as beside their door is the door to the stairway going up to us guys' bedrooms.

The T.V. room has a huge window that is directly above the one in the dining room. We all love to read books in this room, because two walls of it have built in shelves, so it is also the library!

As I just mentioned above, there is a stairway beside the coat closet and powder rooms that goes to the dining room downstairs. It is ten feet wide, and you can look down to the right over the railing and see the laundry room hallway down below. It has ceramic tile on its steps, and the right side is made of glass. And, of course, there is a wood railing on top of the glass that matches the railing on the other side. The soda fountain counter ends at the wall created by this stairway.

In the kitchen, below the stairway coming from the great foyer, is a walk-in closet with lots of shelves for cleaning supplies and pots and pans; the 50-gallon wheeled cart for putting waste basket trash in is in there, as well as the vacuum cleaner. Also, there is a cabinet above the dish washing sinks on the south side of the kitchen for storing dishes in. There is also a narrow floor to ceiling cabinet for spices and condiments between the refrigerators and the doors to the pantry and half-bath that are on the east wall of the kitchen. The stove is in the center of the room, and there is a swinging door to the kitchen beside the dishwashing sinks. This swinging door goes out to the hall going to the game/exercise room.

On the east side of the great foyer upstairs is the very wide square arch that allows you to go into the great room! In fact, it comprises all of that wall which isn't a wall at all, but the widest square arch you ever saw! But there are four pillars in it since, after all, the closets in the master suite are above it!

On the north end of this foyer behind the great room is the door to the seven-car garage. To the left as soon as you go into the garage there is space for the cart that takes groceries downstairs to the pantry on the elevator out in the great foyer. There is a boot washing station beside this space, and it is in the corner of the garage. On two walls of it are hooks to hang rain coats on.

To the right of the door going into the garage from the great foyer there is a door going outside which is handy for anybody who has dirty boots, or shoes after coming in from outside.

I should mention that there is a door going outside from the southwest corner of the great room that goes to a patio with wrought iron furniture, and when you're in the patio you will see a sidewalk along the south side of it. This sidewalk then turns to go along the side of the bedroom wing, and then it goes to the staircase vestibule at the south end of the bedroom wing.

And, as I mentioned earlier, there is another way you can get to Brian and my bedroom suite on the second floor. It is with a stairway going up from the T.V. room hallway. When you open that door in the T.V. room hallway, there is a stairway just like all the other ones in the house. At the top of this stairway, which goes up in a northward direction, the railing turns 180 degrees to be beside the living room and keeps you from falling into the stairwell.

Because the elevator from the laundry room hallway goes to the great foyer and master suite, dirty laundry can be brought downstairs and clean laundry upstairs. And Sarah uses three electric laundry carts to haul everyone's laundry around. These laundry carts are rotated from full to empty and one of them is kept at the bottom of the cart-sized laundry chute coming from Brian and my suite. When that laundry cart is full, Sarah picks it up from a door in the game/exercise room hallway. It gets full quickly because clothes from Brian and my drying racks, as well as Jenny and Chloe's drying racks are thrown into it from dirty clothes closets beside the huge chute! Grandpa and Grandma throw dirty clothes into it from the drying racks in their dirty clothes closet, too, since the cart is actually in their dirty-clothes closet!

The laundry carts that Sarah uses can be rinsed out because there is a hose and a drain in the laundry room.

Sarah also keeps a laundry cart in the dirty-clothes closet in the master suite. And there is a door to this dirty- clothes closet in the foyer that the elevator ends up in at the master suite level.

There are other doors from this foyer on the master suite level that one not only goes into the master suite, but also one that goes into the hallway beside the two bedrooms of Sarah and Johnny's apartment! As also this foyer has a door to the stairway going up to the attics, in addition to the one going into the dirty clothes closet in the master suite. This dirty- clothes closet also has a long hang up rod for dying dirty clothes on!

Since Sarah is going to have a baby, we have hired a retired couple from our church to help her with the clothes washing and cleaning of the house. Their names are James and Gloria and live in Johnny's former apartment.

Sarah now concerns herself with cooking all those awesome meals that she and Johnny have always cooked up! He has also always helped her with the laundry and cleaning of the house when he is not mowing the lawn or plowing snow in the winter.

The Design of Our House:

Great Grandpa Joshua did a good job having our house designed and built in the 1940s. It is a Hansel and Grettel design and all four roofs are steep and the same height. This means there is a lot of space for storage in the attics.

At the south-west corner of the south bedroom wing, the ground starts dropping off very quickly toward the big valley and the creek at the bottom of it. However, at the south end of the patio in front of Grandpa and Grandma's apartment there is a retaining wall with a tall wrought iron fence on top of it. This retaining wall and fence end up going along the south side of the back yard, and then it goes to the southwest corner of it. From there, it goes north across the end of the lawn to the northwest corner, and you can even look down into the valley below! Needless to say, it's an awesome view!

It is the same on the north side. From the northwest corner of the seven-car garage the ground very quickly goes to the creek at the bottom of the big valley.

Just like on the south side, there is a retaining wall that starts at the one-car garage on the north side of Johnny's former apartment. And, of course, the wrought iron fence is on top of this wall also, and it goes to the gate where the dumpster driveway comes into the backyard. Then it continues on the other side of the gate to go to the northwest corner of the backyard.

That retaining wall with a wrought iron fence on top of it that encircles the back yard has two functions, one is that it keeps everybody from falling into the big valley from the backyard, and number two, it keeps people from getting into (and falling into) the backyard from the front lawn level.

The wrought iron fence and retaining wall goes all the way around the backyard, and the beauty of this is that we have yet to lose a croquet ball to the big valley.

The Construction of the House:

When the basement of the house was excavated, a layer of granite was uncovered (Great Grandpa and the engineers knew it was there!) The layer of granite is quite deep, and it became the foundation for the back yard. And this allowed for a small portion of it to stick out over the big valley! (However, the foundation for the west end of the back yard goes way down to the creek and is in actuality a flood wall!)

When construction started, the dumpster driveway was the first thing to be put in. It was necessary for getting all that excess dirt and rock away from the construction area, as well as construction material and equipment to the lower level. So, the dumpster driveway had a very solid bed for putting blacktop on by the time construction ended.

The dumpster driveway goes gradually up the side of the bluff in the form of a terrace and has a very solid retaining wall on the east sides of it with a wrought iron fence on top to keep hikers from falling onto the dumpster driveway; as also there is a not-so high wall on the west side of it.

So during construction, the trucks, equipment and materials had no problem getting to the lower level from the front lawn level.

My Family:

There are eight of us in my family that live in this house. They are: 1 & 2.) Grandpa and Grandma who are awesome neighbors; 3 & 4.) my parents who are the best parent in the world; 5 & 6.) Jenny and Chloe: Jenny is two years younger than I am and Chloe is two years younger than Jenny. 7.) my younger brother, Brian, who is two years younger than Chloe, and 8.) there is me.

I am a senior in hi-school, and Jenny is a sophomore. Chloe is in the 8th grade, and Brian is in 6th grade.

My brother and I get along like Wally and the Beaver, and Jenny tolerates Chloe quite a lot, since it is her Christian obligation to do so.

All four of us are active in our youth groups at church which my grandparents have gone to most of their lives. I say, "most of" because they had to leave their former church because some people came and tried to make the church more Jewish. So my grandparents left and with some others, started a new 'Praise Church'!

The new church now has 500 members, and I love the music there! (I play a base guitar and play in the Praise Band on Sunday morning!)

My parents, Jacob, or Jack, and Celeste, are nice people and we all get along pretty well!!! And my grandparents, Joshua and Susan, are a delight to have as neighbors!!!!! They are my paternal grandparents, and my maternal grandparents, Joseph and Ruth live in Israel. They went there to be missionaries when Joseph retired from the bank that he worked in with Grandpa who was the CEO. Dad is now the CEO.

My great grandfather, Joshua the 1st, bought the bank he worked in, and then Grandpa became president when Great Grandpa retired. Grandpa and Joseph were good friends, because they worked together for so many years. Joseph was vice-president, and then retired early to go into the ministry to Israel! He can even speak Hebrew!!

We are all Messianic Jews, because great grandfather, Joshua, had accepted Jesus Christ in Israel as a teenager, and then immigrated to America!

We have all accepted Jesus Christ as our personal savior, too!

My family goes to Israel at least once a year for

a visit. This year will be the first time since 2019 that we have been able to do that, since we weren't able in 2020 and 2021 due to the Covid 19 pandemic. It will be really nice to see everybody again!